J398. 8.

This book is to be returned on or before the last date stamped below

METHIL 11/2+1

27 JAN 2023

PROJECT

EDUCATIONAL LIBRARY SERVICE
Auchterderran Staff Development & Resources Centre
Woodend Road, Cardenden, Fife. KY5 0NE

D1493749

We...ie

and ...ren

s...

U398.8

Other books of interest from
SCOTTISH CHILDREN'S PRESS and Scottish Cultural Press

SCOTTISH CHILDREN'S PRESS

Classic Children's Games from Scotland
Kendric Ross; 1 899827 12 9

An A–Z of Scots Words for Young Readers
1 899827 03 X

Aiken Drum: a story in Scots for Young Readers
Anne Forsyth; 1 899827 00 5

Kitty Bairdie: a story in Scots for Young Readers
Anne Forsyth; 1899827 01 3

Rashiecoat: a story in Scots for Young Readers
Anne Forsyth; 1 899827 19 6

SCOTTISH CULTURAL PRESS

Teach Yourself Doric: A Course for Beginners
Douglas Kynoch; 1 898218 14 5

Canty and Couthie: Familiar and Forgotten Traditional Scots Poems, Anne Forsyth (ed); 1 898218 04 8

The Midwinter Music: A Scottish Anthology for the Festive Season
Marjory Greig (ed); 1 898218 21 8

To receive complete, up-to-date catalogues
please contact the publisher

First published 1996
SCOTTISH CHILDREN'S PRESS
Unit 14, Leith Walk Business Centre,
130 Leith Walk, Edinburgh, EH6 5DT
Tel: 0131 555 5950

© Fiona Petersen 1996

All rights reserved. No part of this publication may be reproduced, stored in a retrieval system, or transmitted in any form or by any means, electronic, mechanical, photocopying, recording or otherwise without the prior permission of Scottish Children's Press

SCOTTISH CHILDREN'S PRESS is an imprint of
Scottish Cultural Press, PO Box 106, Aberdeen, AB11 7ZE
Tel: 01224 583777 . Fax: 01224 575337

British Library Cataloguing in Publication Data
A catalogue record for this book is available from the British Library

ISBN: 1 899827 17 X

The publisher acknowledges subsidy from the Scottish Arts Council towards the publication of this volume

EDUCATIONAL
LIBRARY SERVICE

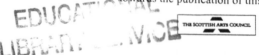

Printed and bound in Great Britain by
Cromwell Press, Melksham, Wiltshire

Scottish Children's Press would like to thank the staff and pupils of Victoria Road Primary School, Aberdeen, for their assistance in the production of this volume.

Contents

1

BAIRN SANGS

1

The wee man came ower the hill,
Chapped at the door
Keeked in
Lifted the sneck
And walked in.

2

Brow, brow, brenty
Eye, eye winkie
Nose, nose, nebbie
Cheek, cheek, cherry
Mou, mou, merry,
Chin, chin, chackie,
Catch a flee, catch a flee.

3

Me broo brinkie
Me eyeo life,
Me bubbly ocean
Me peerie knife,
Me chin cherry
Me trapple kirry, kirry.

Leanne Cowe

4

Tae titly,
Little fitty,
Shin sharpy,
Knee knapy,
Hinchie pinchie,
Wymie bulgy,
Breast berry,
Chin cherry,
Moo merry,
Nose nappy,
Ee winky,
Broo brinky,
Ower the croon,
And awa' wi' it.

5

Hushie-ba, burdie beeton!
Your mammie's gane to Seaton,
For to buy a lammie's skin,
To wrap your bonnie boukie in.

Bye, babie buntin',
Your daddie's gane a-huntin';
Your mammie's gane to buy a skin
To row the babie buntin' in.

6

O can ye sew cushions,
Or can ye sew sheets,
An' can ye sing ba-loo-loo,
When the bairn greets?
An' hee and ba, birdie,
An' hee and ba, lamb;
An' hee and ba, birdie,
My bonnie wee man!

   Hee O, wee O, what'll I do wi' you?
   Black is the life that I lead wi' you,
   Owre mony o' you, little to gie you;
   Hee O, wee O, what'll I do wi' you?

Now hush-a-ba, lammie,
An' hush-a-ba, dear,
Now hush-a-ba, lammie,
Thy minnie is here.
The wild wind is ravin',
Thy minnie's heart's sair,
The wild wind is ravin',
An' ye dinna care.

   Hee O, wee O   etc

Sing ba-la-loo, lammie,
Sing ba-la-loo, dear,
Does wee lammie ken
That his daddie's no here?
Ye're rocking fu' sweetly
On mammie's warm knee,
But daddie's a-rockin'
Upon the saut sea.

   Hee O, wee O   etc

O I hung thy cradle
On yon holly top,
An' aye as the wind blew
Thy cradle did rock,
An' hush-a-ba, baby,
O ba-lilly-loo,
An' hee an' ba, birdie,
My bonnie wee doo!

   Hee O, wee O   etc

Emma Tarburn

4

7

(playing with baby's feet, making them go up and down and over each other, saying the following verse)

This is Willie Walker, and that's Tam Sim,
He ca'd him to a feast, and he ca'd him;
And he sticket him wi' the spit, and he sticket him,
And he owre him, and he owre him,
And he owre him, and he owre him, etc
Till day brak.

or

'Feetikin, feetikin,
When will ye gang?'
'When the nichts turn short,
And the days turn lang.
I'll toddle and gang, toddle and gang,'...*etc*

8

Dance to your daddie,
My bonnie laddie,
Dance to your daddie, my bonnie lamb!
And ye'll get a fishie
In a little dishie—
Ye'll get a fishie when the boat comes hame!

Dance to your daddie,
My bonnie laddie,
Dance to your daddie, my bonnie lamb!
And ye'll get a coatie,
And a pair o' breekies—
Ye'll get a whippie and a supple Tam!

9

insert the baby's name in the appropriate place

The craws hae killed the poussie, O,
The craws hae killed the poussie, O,
The mickle cat sat down and grat
In ——'s wee bit housie, O.

10

Hush-a-bye baby,
Lie still an sleep soun',
Your mammie's awa tae the mill;
An' she'll no be hame,
Till the licht o the mune,
Sae hush-a-bye baby,
Lie still.

11 Tom Thumb

I got a little manikin, I set him on my thoomiken;
I saddled him, I bridled him, and sent him to the
 tooniken;
I coffed a pair o' garters to tie his little hosiken;
I coffed a pocket-napkin to dicht his little nosiken;
I sent him to the garden to fetch a pund o' sage,
And fand him in the kitchen neuk kissing little Madge!

Mark Smith & Darren Smith

12

Using the fingers:

Thumbkin brak the barn,
Lickpot stealt the corn,
Langman carried it awa'
Berrybarn stood and saw,
Wee Pirly Winkie paid for a'.

13

One, two, three, a-leerie,
I spy Bella Peerie,
Sittin' on a basket cheerie,
Eatin' jelly babies.

14

I've a kisty
I've a creel
I've a baggie
Fou o' meal.

I've a doggie
At the door
One, two,
Three, four.

15

Eentie teentie terry erry ram tam toosh,
Go to the cellar, catch a wee, wee moose,
Cut it up in slices, fry it in the pan,
Mind and leave the gravy for the wee fat man!

16

A laird, a lord, a rich man, a thief,
A piper, a drummer, a stealer o beef.

17

Eatum, peatum, potum, pie,
Babylonie, stickum, stie,
Dog's tail, hog's snout,
I'm in, you're out.

18

Eerie, orie, owre the dam,
Fill your poke and let us gang;
Black fish and white trout,
Eerie, orie, you're out.

19

Eetle ottle, black bottle
Eetle ottle out,
If ye want a piece and jam,
Please step out.

Amanda McKay & Clair Stephen

20

Ease, ose, man's nose;
Cauld parritch, pease brose.

21

Willie Warstle, auld Carle,
Dottered, dune, and doited bodie,
Feeds his weans on calf's lugs,
Soups o' brose, and draps o' crowdie.

2
PEOPLE

22 Katie Beardie

Katie Beardie had a coo,
Black and white about the mou';
Wasna that a dentie coo?
Dance, Katie Beardie!

Katie Beardie had a hen,
Cackled but and cackled ben;
Wasna that a dentie hen?
Dance, Katie Beardie!

Katie Beardie had a cock,
That could spin backin' rock;
Wasna that a dentie cock?
Dance, Katie Beardie!

Katie Beardie had a grice,
It could skate upon the ice;
Wasna that a dentie grice?
Dance, Katie Beardie!

23 Tam o' the Linn

Tam o' the linn cam up the gait,
Wi' twenty puddings on a plate,
And every pudding had a pin,
'We'll eat them a',' quo Tam o' the linn.

Tam o' the Linn

Nicola Leighton

Tam o' the linn had nae breeks tae wear,
He coft him a sheep-skin to make him a pair,
The fleshy side out, the woolly side in,
'It's a fine summer cleeding,' quo Tam o' the linn.

Tam o' the linn, he had three bairns,
They fell in the fire, in each other's arms;
'Oh,' quo the boonmost, 'I've got a het skin;'
'It's better below,' quo Tam o' the linn.

Tam o' the linn gaed to the moss,
To seek a stable to his horse;
The moss was open, and Tam fell in,
'I've stabled mysel',' quo Tam o' the linn.

24 Babbity Bowster

Wha learned you to dance
Babbity Bowster, Babbity Bowster,
Wha learned you to dance
Babbity Bowster brawly?

'My minnie learned me to dance
Babbity Bowster, Babbity Bowster,
My minnie learned me to dance
Babbity Bowster brawly.'

Wha ga'e you the keys to keep,
Babbity Bowster, Babbity Bowster,
Wha ga'e you the keys to keep,
Babbity Bowster brawly?

'My minnie ga'e me the keys to keep,
Babbity Bowster, Babbity Bowster,
'My minnie ga'e me the keys to keep,
Babbity Bowster brawly.'

25 Aiken Drum

There cam a man to our town, to our town, to our town,
There cam a man to our town, and his name was Willy Wood.
And he played upon a razor, a razor, a razor,
And he played upon a razor, and his name was Willy Wood.

His hat was made o' the guid roast beef, the guid roast beef, the guid roast beef,
His hat was made o' the guid roast beef, and his name was Willy Wood.

His coat was made o' the haggis bag, the haggis bag, the haggis bag,
His coat was made o' the haggis bag, and his name was Willy Wood.

His buttons were made o' the baubee baps, the baubee baps, the baubee baps,
His buttons were made o' the baubee baps, and his name was Willy Wood.

But another man cam to the town, cam to the town, cam to the town,
But another man cam to the town, and they ca'd him Aiken Drum.
And he played upon a ladle, a ladle, a ladle,
He played upon a ladle, and they ca'd him Aiken Drum.

Suzanne Esson

10

And he ate up the guid roast beef, the guid roast beef,
   the guid roast beef,
And he ate up the guid roast beef, and his name was
   Aiken Drum.

And he ate up the haggis bag *etc*

And he ate up the baubee baps *etc*

26 The Wee Wifie

There was a wee wifie row't up in a blanket,
Nineteen times as high as the moon;
And what did she there I canna declare,
For in her oxter she carried the sun.
'Wee wifie, wee wifie, wee wifie,' quo I,
'O what are ye doin' up there sae hie?'
'I'm blawin' the cauld clouds out o' the sky.'
'Weel dune, weel dune, wee wifie!' quo I.

27

Matthew, Mark, Luke, John,
Haud the horse till I loup on;
Haud it fast, and haud it sure,
Till I get owre the misty muir.

28 The Three Kings

There were three kings cam frae the East;
They spiered in ilka clachan;
'O, which is the way to Bethlehem,
My bairns, sae bonnily lachin'?'

O neither young nor old could tell;
They trailed till their feet were weary.
They followed a bonny gowden starn,
That shone in the lift sae cheery.

The starn stude ower the ale-hoose byre
Whaur the stable gear was hinging'.
The owsen mooed, the bairnie grat,
The Kings begoud their singin'.

29 The Candy Man

The Candy Man was guid tae me
He took me up an' gied me tea,
Tea an' toast an' a wee bit ham,
'Twas afa good o' the Candy Man.

30 Willie Winkie

(William Miller 1810–1872, Glasgow)

Wee Willie Winkie rins through the toun,
Upstairs and doon stairs in his nicht-gown,
Tirling at the window, crying at the lock:
'Are the weans in their bed, for it's now ten o'clock?'

'Hey, Willie Winkie, are ye comin' ben?
The cat's singing grey thrums to the sleeping hen,
The dog's spelder'd on the floor, and disna gi'e a cheep,
But here's a waukrife laddie that winna fa' asleep.'

Onything but sleep, you rogue! glow'ring like the moon,
Rattling in an airn jug wi' an airn spoon,
Rumbling, tumbling round about, crawing like a cock,
Skirling like a kenna-what, wauk'ning sleeping folk.

'Hey, Willie Winkie!'—the wean's in a creel!
Wambling aff a bodie's knee like a very eel,
Rugging at the cat's lug, and raveling a' her thrums—
'Hey, Willie Winkie!'—see, there he comes.

Wearied is the mither that has a stoorie wean,
A wee stumpie stoussie, that canna rin his lane,
That has a battle aye wi' sleep before he'll close an e'e—
But a kiss frae aff his rosy lips gi'es strength anew to me.

Kelly Main

31 John Frost

(David Wingate)

Oh, mither, John Frost cam' yestreen,
An' owre a' the garden he's been;
    He's on the kail-stocks,
    And my twa printed frocks,
That Mary left out on the green,
    Yestreen,
John Frost fand them oot on the green.

An' he's been on the trees, the auld loon,
An' heaps o' brown leaves shooken doun',
    He's been fleein' a' nicht,
    Frae the dark to the licht,
An' missed nae a house in the toun,
    The auld loon —
He's missed nae a house in the toun.

An' mither, he's killed every flee—
Noo ane on wa's ye'll no' see;
    On the windows there's nane,
    For the last livin' ane
Fell down frae the rape in oor tea,
    Puir thing! —
Just drappit dound dead in our tea.

An', mither, the path's frostit a';
If ye gang the least fast ye just fa';
    Oh, you ne'er saw sic fun!
    I got ae curran' bun,
An' wee Annie Kenzie got twa—
    Daft wee thing;
She just slade a wee bit an' got twa.

An' my auntie her een couldna close,
For she said her auld bluid he just froze;
    He cam' in below the claes,
    An' he nippet oor taes—
An' he maist ta'en awa' Bobby's nose,
    Puir wee man!
Sure he couldna do wantin' his nose.

An' my uncle was chitterin' to daith,
An' John Frost wadna let him get braith,
    An' the fire wadna heat
    Uncle's twa starvin' feet,
Till the soles o' his socks were burned baith,
    Birslet broon,
An' the reek comin' oot o' them baith.

But what brings John Frost here ava,
Wi' his frost an' his cranreugh an' snaw?
    It's a bonny-like thing!
    He just waff't his lang wing,
An' a' oor wee flowers flew awa',
    Every ane;
An' Ross's red dawlies an' a'.

An', mither, he gangs through the street,
Just looking for weans wi' bare feet;
    An' he nips at their heels,
    An' the skin aff them peels,
An' thinks it fine fun when they greet,
    The auld loon;
He nips them the mair when they greet.

Wi' his capers the folk shouldna thole,
D'ye ken? He breathed in through a hole
    Whare a wee lassie lay,
    An' she dee't the next day,
An' they laid her dound in the kirk-hole,
    Puir wee lamb!
An' covered her in the kirk-hole.

But guess what my auntie tell't me?
She says the wee weans, when they dee,
    Flee awa' owre the moon,
    An' need nae claes nor shoon,
To a place where John Frost they'll nae see,
    Far awa'—
To a place where John Frost daurna be.

Stephen Ross

An' she says oor wee Katie gaed there,
An' she'll never be hoastin' nae mair,
   Sure we'll gang there ana'—
   We'll flee up an' no fa'—
An' we'll see her just in her wee chair—
   An' she'll lauch
In her bonnie wee red cushioned chair!

32 The Piper o' Dundee

And wasna he a roguey,
A roguey, a roguey,
And wasna he a roguey,
The piper o' Dundee?

The piper came to our town,
To our town, to our town,
The piper came to our town,
And he played bonnilie.

He played a spring the laird to please,
A spring brent new frae yont the seas;
And then he ga'e his bags a heeze,
And played anither key.

33 Johnnie Smith, my Falla Fine

(Robert Grant, Peterhead, 1818)

'Johnnie Smith, my falla fine,
Can ye shoe this horse o' mine?'
'Weel I wat, an' that I can,
Jest as weel as ony man.

'Put a bittie on a tae,
Gars a horsie spur a brae;
Put a bittie on a heel
Gars a horsie trot weel.

'Gin ye're for the Hieland road
Ye maun hae yer beast weel shod;
An' I'm the man can do it weel,
Wi' best o' airn an' o' steel.

'Wha like me can drive a nail,
Dress a beast, an' busk his tail?
Nane in a' the country roun'
Like Johnnie Smith o' Turra toun.

'The road is far I hae to ride,
Frae Turra toun tae Gelder side;
But gin ye're canny wi' my mear,
I will roose ye far an' near.'

'Ye may roose me as ye like,
To Hieland laird or tinkler tyke;
But five white shillin's is my fee;
Gin it please ye we will gree.'

'Gree, my man! 'tween you an' me
There sall never be a plea;
Wha wad grudge to pay a croun
To Johnnie Smith o' Turra toun?'

Johnnie shod my mear richt weel,
Tipp'd ilk shoe wi' bits o' steel'
An' ere the sun gaed doun that nicht,
I saw Balmoral's towers in sicht.

Hurrah! the Smith o' Turra toun,
Tho' a gey camstairie loun,
Nane like him can drive a nail,
Pare a hoof, or busk a tail.

34 Jockie Smith

Jockie Smith, my fellow fine
Can ye shoe this horse o' mine?
Yes indeed an' that I can,
Jist as weel as ony man!
Ca' a nail intae the tae
To gar the pownie clim' the brae!
Ca' a nail intae the heel
To gar the pownie scamper weel!
There's a nail an' there's a brod
An there's a pownie weel shod.
Weel shod, weel shod!
A weel shod pownie!

35

'Whistle, whistle, auld wife,
An' ye'se get a hen.'
'I wadna whistle,' quo' the wife,
'Though ye wad gie me ten.'

'Whistle, whistle, auld wife,
An' ye'se get a cock.'
'I wadna whistle,' quo the wife,
'Though ye'd gie me a flock.'

'Whistle, whistle, auld wife,
An' ye'se get a goun.'
'I wadna whistle,' quo the wife,
'For the best ane i' the toun.'

'Whistle, whistle auld wife,
An' ye'se get a coo.'
'I wadna whistle,' quo the wife,
'Though ye wad gie me two.'

'Whistle, whistle, auld wife,
An' ye'se get a man.'
'Wheeple-whawple,' quo' the wife,
'I'll whistle as I can.'

36 Queen Mary, Queen Mary

Queen Mary, Queen Mary, my age is sixteen,
My father's a farmer on yonder green,
With plenty of money to dress me fu' braw,
But nae bonnie laddie will tak' me awa'.
One morning I rose, and I looked in the glass,
Says I to myself, I'm a handsome young lass;
My hands by my side and I gave a ha! ha!
Yet there's nae bonnie laddie will tak' me awa'.

Louise Nicol

3

WEATHER, SEASONS, NATURE

37

Mony hawes
Mony snaws

38

Mony a frost and mony a thowe,
Soon maks mony a rotten yowe.

39 early winter

An air' winter,
A sair winter.

40

Februar, an ye be fair,
The hoggs 'll mend, and naething pair;
Februar, an ye be foul,
The hoggs 'll die in ilka pool.

41

February, fill the dike,
Be it black, or be it white!
It it be white, it's the better to like.

Sara Khellaf & Jena McArthur

'Half past ten, dingin on o rain...' Corrine Moffat

42

Leap year
Was never a good sheep year.

43 Candlemas

(2 February)

If Candlemas-day be dry and fair,
The half o' winter's to come and mair;
If Candlemas-day be wet and foul,
The half o' winter's gane at Yule.

44

March borrowed from April
Three days, and they were ill;
The first o' them was wind and weet;
The second o' them was snaw and sleet;
The third o' them was sic a freeze,
It froze the birds' nebs to the trees.

(refers to the last three days of March which were considered highly superstitous during the seventeenth century)

45

Mist in May, and heat in June,
Maks the harvest richt sune.

46

March dust and May sun,
Makes corn white, and maidens dun. *(Perthshire)*

March dust and March's wind,
Bleaches as weel as simmer's sun. *(Clydesdale)*

March water and May sun,
Makes claes clear, and maidens dun. *(Mearns)*

47

Till May be out
Change na a clout.

48

The south wind – heat and plenty,
The west wind – fish and cheese,
The north wind – cauld and stormy,
The east wind – fruit on trees.

49

Half past ten, dingin on o rain,
Half past twa, dingin on snaw.

50 A Star

I had a little sister, they called her Peep-Peep,
She waded the waters so deep, deep, deep;
She climbed up the mountains so high, high, high;
And, poor little thing, she had but one eye.

51

Rainy, rainy rattlestanes,
Dinna rain on me;
But rain on Johnnie Groat's hoose,
Far across the sea.

52

The moon shines bright,
And the stars gie a light,
We'll see to kiss a bonny lass
At ten o'clock at night!

53

Auld moon mist
Ne'er died o' thirst

(foggy weather in the last quarter of the moon is thought to predict rain)

Kelly Duncan

54

About the moon there is a brugh;
The weather will be cauld and rough.

(a halo around the moon may well precede wet weather)

55

If the oak's before the ash
Then you'll only get a splash;
If the ash precedes the oak,
Then you may expect a soak.

56 wind

East and wast,
The sign of a blast;
North and south,
The sign of drouth.

57 sky colour

The evening red, and the morning gray,
Are the tokens of a bonnie day.

58

Wild geese, wild geese, ganging tae the sea,
Good weather it will be.
Wild geese, wild geese, ganging tae the hill.
The weather it will spill. *(Moray)*

Bryan McCaffrey

23

59

Hips and haws are very good meat,
But bread and butter is better to eat.

60 different kinds of milk

Sweet milk, sour milk,
Thick milk, thin;
Blased milk, bladded milk,
Milk new come in;
Milk milket aff milk,
Milk in a pig.
New-calved kye's milk,
Sour kirnie whig.

61 Glasgow's Coat of Arms

This is the tree that never grew;
This is the bird that never flew;
This is the bell that never rang;
And this is the fish that never swam.

62

Fin the mist comes fae the sea
Dry weather it will be,
Fin the mist comes fae the hill,
Ye'll get watter tae yer mill.

Jovanna Driacic

4

BEASTIES!

63

The horny gollach's an awesome beast,
Souple an scaly;
He has twa horns an a hantle o feet
An a forkie tailie.

64

The cuckoo's a bonny bird,
He sings as he flies;
He brings us good tidings;
He tells us no lies.

He drinks the cold water,
To keep his voice clear;
And he'll come again
In the spring of the year.

65

Snailie snailie, pit oot yer horn,
An tell me it'll be a fine day the morn.

Melanie Brown

66

Sea gull, sea gull, sit on the sand;
It's never good weather when you're on the land.

67

Mousie, mousie, come to me;
The cat's awa frae hame;
Mousie, mousie, come to me,
I'll use you kind, and mak you tame.

68 Cat purring

Dirdum drum,
Three threads and a thrum,
Thrum gray, thrum gray.

69

Lingle, lingle, lang tang,
Our cat's dead!
What did she dee wi'?
Wi' a sair head!

Simone Barbour

A' you that kent her
When she was alive,
Come to her burial
Atween four and five.

70

Poussie, poussie, baudrons,
Where hae ye been?
'I've been at London,
Seeing the queen!'

Poussie, poussie, baudrons,
What got ye there?
'I got a guid fat mousikie,
Rinning up a stair!'

Poussie, poussie, baudrons,
What did ye do wi't?
'I put it in my meal-poke,
To eat it to my bread!'

Kathleen McGhee

27

71 The mole

The moudiewort, the moudiewort,
The mumpin' beast the moudiewort;
The craws hae pykit the moudiewort,
The puir wee beast the moudiewort.

72 The cattie sits in the kiln-ring spinning

The cattie sits in the kiln-ring,
Spinning, spinning;
And by came a little wee mousie,
Rinning, rinning.

'O what's that you're spinning, my loesome,
Loesome lady?'
'I'm spinning a sark to my young son,'
Said she, said she.

'Weel mot he brook it, my loesome,
Loesome lady.'
'Gif he dinna brook it weel, he may brook it ill,'
Said she, said she.

'I soopit my house, my loesome,
Loesome lady.'
' 'Twas a sign ye didna sit amang dirt then,'
Said she, said she.

'I fand twall pennies, my winsome,
Winsome lady.'
' 'Twas a sign ye warna sillerless,'
Said she, said she.

'I gaed to the market, my loesome,
Loesome lady.'
' 'Twas a sign ye didna sit at hame then,'
Said she, said she.

'I coft a sheepie's head, my winsome,
Winsome lady.'
' 'Twas a sign ye warna kitchenless,'
Said she, said she.

'I put it in my pottie to boil, my loesome,
Loesome lady.'
' 'Twas a sign ye didna eat it raw,'
Said she, said she.

'I put it in my winnock to cool, my winsome,
Winsome lady.'
' 'Twas a sign ye didna burn your chafts, then,'
Said she, said she.

'By came a cattie, and ate it a' up, my loesome,
Loesome lady.'
'And sae will I you — *worrie, worrie — gnash, gnash*,'
Said she, said she.

73 The Frog and Mouse

There lived a Puddy in a well,
        Cuddy alane, cuddy alane;
There lived a Puddy in a well,
        Cuddy alane and I.
There was a Puddy in a well,
And a mousie in a mill;
Kickmaleerie, cowden down,
Cuddy alane and I.

Puddy he'd a-wooin' ride,
        Cuddy alane, cuddy alane;
Puddy he'd a-wooin' ride,
        Cuddy alane and I;
Puddy he'd a-wooin' ride,
Sword and pistol by his side.
Kickmaleerie, cowden down,
Cuddy alone and I.

Puddy came to the mouse's wonne:
        Cuddy alane, cuddy alane;
Puddy came to the mouse's wonne:
        Cuddy alane and I;
Puddy came to the mouse's wonne:
'Mistress Mouse, are you within?'
Kickmaleerie, cowden down,
Cuddy alane and I.

'Yes, kind sir, I am within;
        Cuddy alane, cuddy alane;
'Yes, kind sir, I am within;
        Cuddy alane and I;
'Yes, kind sir, I am within;
Saftly do I sit and spin.'
Kickmaleerie, cowden down,
Cuddy alane and I.

'Madam, I am come to woo;
        Cuddy alane, cuddy alane;

'Madam, I am come to woo;
    Cuddy alane and I;
'Madam, I am come to woo;
Marriage I must have of you.'
Kickmaleerie, cowden down,
Cuddy alane and I.

'Marriage I will grant you nane,
    Cuddy alane, cuddy alane;
'Marriage I will grant you nane,
    Cuddy alane and I;
'Marriage I will grant you nane,
Till Uncle Rottan he cames hame.'
Kickmaleerie, cowden down,
Cuddy alane and I.

Uncle Rottan's now come hame,
    Cuddy alane, cuddy alane;
Uncle Rottan's now come hame,
    Cuddy alane and I;
Uncle Rottan's now come hame,
'Fye, gar busk the bride alang!'
Kickmaleerie, cowden down,
Cuddy alane and I.

Lord Rottan sat at the head o' the table,
    Cuddy alane, cuddy alane;
Lord Rottan sat at the head o' the table,
    Cuddy alane and I;
Lord Rottan sat at the head o' the table,
Because he was baith stout and able.
Kickmaleerie, cowden down,
Cuddy alane and I.

Wha is't that sits next the wa',
    Cuddy alane, cuddy alane;
Wha is't that sits next the wa',
    Cuddy alane and I;
Wha is't that sits next the wa',
But Lady Mouse, baith jimp and sma'?
Kickmaleerie, cowden down,
Cuddy alane and I.

Martin Main

What is't that sits next the bride,
    Cuddy alane, cuddy alane;
What is't that sits next the bride,
    Cuddy alane and I;
What is't that sits next the bride,
But the sola Puddy wi' his yellow side?
Kickmaleerie, cowden down,
Cuddy alane and I.

Syne came the Deuk but and the Drake,
    Cuddy alane, cuddy alane;
Syne came the Deuk but and the Drake,
    Cuddy alane and I;
Syne came the Deuk but and the Drake,
The Deuk took the Puddy, and gart him squaik.
Kickmaleerie, cowden down,
Cuddy alane and I.

Then came in the fine grey Cat,
    Cuddy alane, cuddy alane;
Then came in the fine grey Cat,
    Cuddy alane and I;
Then came in the fine grey Cat,
Wi' all the kittlins on her back:
Kickmaleerie, cowden down,
Cuddy alane and I.

The Puddy he swam down the brook,
    Cuddy alane, cuddy alane;
The Puddy he swam down the brook,
    Cuddy alane and I;
The Puddy he swam down the brook,
The Drake he catched him in his fluke.
Kickmaleerie, cowden down,
Cuddy alane and I

The Cat he pu'd Lord Rottan down,
    Cuddy alane, cuddy alane;
The Cat he pu'd Lord Rottan down,
    Cuddy alane and I;
The Cat he pu'd Lord Rottan down,
The kittlins they did claw his crown.
Kickmaleerie, cowden down,
Cuddy alane and I.

But Lady Mouse, baith jimp and sma'.
Crept into a hole beneath the wa';
'Squeak!' quo she, 'I'm weel awa'!'
Kickmaleerie, cowden down,
Cuddy alane and I.

74

Incy wincy spider
Clambered up the spout,
Down came the rain
And washed poor spider out.

Out came the sun
And dried up all the rain.
Incy wincy spider,
Climbed the spout again.

Tracy Towler

75

Cushy cow, bonny, let down thy milk,
And I'll gie you a gown o' silk;
A gown o' silk and a silver tee,
If thou will let down thy milk to me.

76 Magpies

One's sorrow—two's mirth;
Three's a wedding—four's death;
Five a blessing—six hell;
Seven's the deil's ain sel'!

77 White Feet in Horses

If he has *one*, buy him;
If he has *two*, try him;
If he has *three*, look about him;
If he has *four*, come without him.

78 Eel

Eelie, eelie, ator,
Cast a knot upon your tail,
And I'll throw you in the water.

79

Eelie, eelie, cast your knot,
And ye'll get back to your water pot.

80 Ladybird

Lady, Lady Landers,
Lady, Lady Landers,
Take up your coats about your head,
And fly away to Flanders.

81 The crow

On the first of March,
The craws begin to search;
By the first of April,
They are sitting still;
By the first of May,
They're a' flown away;
Croupin' greedy back again,
Wi' October's wind and rain.

Sarah Main

82 The Twa Bumbees

Charles Spence (1779–1869)

There were twa bumbees met on a twig,
Fim-fam, fiddle-faddle, fum, fizz!
Said: 'Whaur will we gang our byke tae big?'
Tig-a-leery, twig-a-leery, bum, bizz!
The modest miss, being rather shy,
Twigg'd round her head and look'd awry,
And gae her dandy nae reply
But 'Tig-a-leery, twig-a-leery, bum, bizz!'

'O! we will gang to yon sunny bank,
Fim-fam, fiddle-faddle, fum, fizz!
Whaur the flowers bloom fair, and the fog grows rank,
Tig-a-leery, twig-a-leery, bum, bizz!'
They sought the bank frae side to side,
In every hole baith straucht and wide,
But nane they saw could please the bride,
Tig-a-leery, twig-a-leery, bum, bizz!

When they had sought frae noon till six,
Fim-fam, fiddle-faddle, fum, fizz!
And on nae place their choice could fix;
Tig-a-leery, twig-a-leery, bum, bizz!
They saw a hole beneath a tree,
'O! this our dwelling place shall be,'
They said, and entered cheerfully,
Tig-a-leery, twig-a-leery, bum, bizz!

Jenny Wren cam hame at night,
Fim-fam, fiddle-faddle, fum, fizz!
And, O! but she got an unco fright,
Tig-a-leery, twig-a-leery, bum, bizz!
She entered in, ne'er dreading harm,
When in her chamber, snug and warm,
The roving pair rang the alarm—
'Tig-a-leery, twig-a-leery, bum, bizz!'

Anthony Walker

34

Jenny Wren, bein' smit wi' fear,
Fim-fam, fiddle-faddle, fum, fizz!
Flew aff, and ne'er again cam near,
Tig-a-leery, twig-a-leery, bum, bizz!
Quoth the gudewife to the gudeman,
'When night her mantle has withdrawn,
And Phœbus shines upon the lawn,
Tig-a-leery, twig-a-leery, bum, bizz!

'We'll gather honey from each flower,
Fim-fam, fiddle-faddle, fum, fizz!
And when the night begins to lower,
Tig-a-leery, twig-a-leery, bum, bizz!
'We'll hither hie, and here we'll meet,
All shielded from the wind and weet,
And a' night lang enjoy the sweet,
Tig-a-leery, twig-a-leery, bum, bizz!'

They hadna been lang beneath the tree,
Fim-fam, fiddle-faddle, fum, fizz?
When out cam' bumbees, ane, twa, three,
Tig-a-leery, twig-a-leery, bum, bizz!
Quoth Mr Bum to Mrs Bee,
'O! had ye a' these bees by me!'
Whilst jealousy lurked in his e'e,
Tig-a-leery, twig-a-leery, bum, bizz!

Quoth Mrs Bee to Mr Bum,
Fim-fam, fiddle-faddle, fum, fizz!
'They're a' as like you's mum's like mum,
Tig-a-leery, twig-a-leery, bum, bizz!
'I cowed the horns frae aff your brow.'
Quoth Mr Bum, 'O, wow, wow, wow!
And had I horns then to cowe?'
Tig-a-leery, twig-a-leery, bum, bizz!

O! a' ye bumbees, whaure'er ye be,
Fim-fam, fiddle-faddle, fum, fizz!
I pray a warning tak' by me,
Tig-a-leery, twig-a-leery, bum, bizz!
Far rather lead a single life
Than wed a wayward, wanton wife,
Wha'll cause you meikle dule and strife,
Tig-a-leery, twig-a-leery, bum, bizz!

83 The Auld Man's Mare's Dead

(Patie Birnie 16??–17??, Kinghorn, Fife)

The auld man's mare's dead;
The puir man's mare's dead;
The auld man's mare's dead,
A mile aboon Dundee.

There was hay to ca', and lint to lead,
A hunder hotts o' muck tae spread,
And peats and truffs and a' to lead—
And yet the jaud to dee!

She had the fiercie and the fleuk,
The wheezloch and the wanton yeuk;
On ilka knee she had a breuk—
What ail'd the beast to dee?

The auld man's mare's dead;
The puir man's mare's dead;
The peats, and neeps, and a' to lead,
And she is gane—wae's me!

She was lang-tooth'd and blench-lippit,
Heam-hough'd and haggis-fittit,
Lang-neckit, chandler-chaftit,
The yet the jaud to dee!

She was cut-luggit, painch-lippit,
Steel-wamet, staincher-fittit,
Chandler-chaftit, lang-neckit,
And yet the brute did dee!

The Auld man's Mare's DEAD

Ryan Reid & Michael Mowat

The auld man's mare's dead;
The puir man's mare's dead;
The auld man's mare's dead,
A better ne'er did dee.

The puir man's head's sair,
Wi' greetin' for his gude grey mare;
He's like to dee himsel' wi' care,
Aside the green kirk-yard.

He's thinkin' on the by-gane days,
And a' her douce and canny ways;
And how his ain gudewife, auld Bess,
Micht maist as weel been spared.

The auld man's mare's dead;
The puir man's mare's dead;
The auld man's mare's dead,
A mile aboon Dundee.

84

Dingle, dingle dousy,
The cat's at the well;
The dog's awa to Musselburgh
To buy the bairn a bell.
Greet, greet, bairnie,
And ye'll get a bell;
If ye dinna greet faster,
I'll keep it to mysel'!

85

Jean, Jean, Jean
The cat's at the cream,
Suppin' wi' her fore-feet,
And glowrin' wi' her een!

86 The Three Craws

Three craws sat upon a wa', sat upon a wa', sat upon a
    wa'
Three craws sat upon a wa', on a cold and frosty
    mornin'.

The first craw was greetin for his maw, greetin for his
    maw, greetin for his maw,
The first craw was greetin for his maw, on a cold and
    frosty mornin'.

The second craw couldna flee at a', couldna flee at a',
    couldna flee at a',
The second craw couldna flee at a', on a cold and frosty
    mornin'.

The third craw fell and skint his jaw, fell and skint his
    jaw, fell and skint his jaw,
The third craw fell and skint his jaw, on a cold and
    frosty mornin'.

The fourth craw, well he wasna there at a', wasna there
  at a', wasna there at a',
The fourth craw wasna there at a', on a cold and frosty
  mornin'.

That's a' we ken aboot the craws, ken aboot the craws,
  ken aboot the craws,
That's a' we ken aboot the craws, on a cold and frosty
  mornin'.

87 My Dragon

(George Donald, 1800–1851, Glasgow)

The hip's on the brier, and the haw's on the thorn,
The primrose is wither'd, and yellow the corn;
The shearers will be soon on Capilrig brae,
Sae I'll aff to the hills wi' my dragon the day!

The wind it comes snelly, and scatters the leaves,
John Frost on the windows a fairy web weaves;
The robin is singing, and black is the slae,
Sae I'll aff to the hills wi' my dragon the day!

I've bought me a string that will reach to the moon,
I wish I could rise wi't the white clouds aboon,
And see the wee stars as they glitter and play!—
Let me aff to the hills wi' my dragon the day!

88

Fa's that ringing at my door bell?
A wee wee cat that's nae very well.
Rub its little nosey wi' a bit o' mutton fat,
For that's the best cure for a wee pussy cat.

Scott Middleton

5

HUMOUR

89

I went tae the pictures tomorra
I took a front seat at the back,
I fell frae the pit to the gallery
And broke a front bone at the back.
A lady she gied me some chocolate,
I ate it and gied her it back.
I phoned for a taxi and walked it,
An that's why I niver cam back.

90

The minister in the pulpit.
He couldnae say his prayers,
He laughed and he giggled
And he fell doon the stairs.
The stairs gave a crack
And he broke his humphy back,
And a the congregation
Went 'Quack, quack, quack!'

91

Skinny malinky long legs, umbrella feet,
Went tae the pictures and couldnae find a seat.
He got the bus hame and widnae pay his fare,
So the rotten auld conductor kicked him doon the stair.

92

Come a riddle, come a riddle, come a rot, tot, tot
A roun, roun man in a red, red coat;
A staff in his hand, and a stane in his throat,
Come a riddle, come a riddle, come a rot, tot, tot.
a cherry

93

A ha'penny here, and a ha'penny there,
Fourpence-ha'penny and a ha'penny mair;
A ha'penny wat, and a ha'penny dry,
Fourpence-ha'penny and a ha'penny forby;
How much is that?   *a shilling*

94

Wee man o' leather
Gaed through the heather,
Through a rock, through a reel,
Through an auld spinning wheel;
Through a sheep-shank bane;
Sic a man was never seen.   *a beetle*

95

A beautiful lady in a garden was laid,
Her beauty was fair as the sun,
In one hour of her life she became a man's wife,
And she died before she was born.   *Eve*

96

Lang syne, when geese were swine,
And turkeys chewed tobacco,
And birds biggit their nests in auld men's beards,
And mowdies del't potatoes.

97

In a loud voice:

Auld wife, auld wife,
Will ye go a-shearing?
'Speak a little louder, sir;
I'm unco dull o' hearing.'

In a quieter tone:

Auld wife, auld wife,
Wad ye tak a kiss?
'Yes, indeed, I will sir—
It wadna be amiss.'

98

There was a wee bit wifie,
Who lived in a shoe,
She had so many bairns,
She kenn'd na what tae do.
She gaed to the market
To buy a sheep head;
When she came back,
They were all lying dead.
She went to the wright
To get them a coffin;
When she came back
They were all lying laughing!
She gaed up the stair,
To ring the bell;
The bell-rope broke,
And down she fell.

99 The Ram o' Bervie

As I went up to Bervie
Upon a market day,
I saw the fattest ram, sir,
That ever was fed on hay.

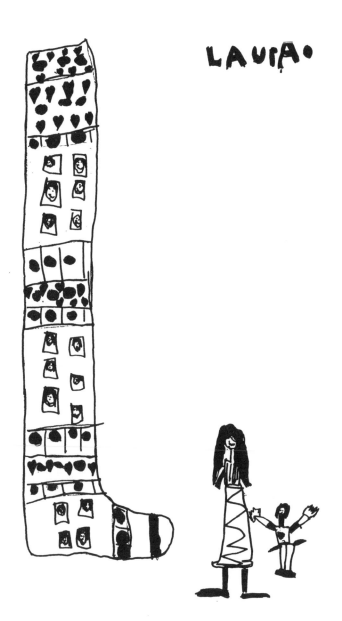

Laura Fullarton

41

Singing hey dingle derby
Hey dingle day;
This was the greatest ram, sir,
That ever was fed on hay.

The ram it had a foot, sir,
Whereon to sit or stand;
And when it laid it down, sir,
It covered an acre of land.

Singing hey.... *etc.*

The ram it had a horn, sir,
That reached up to the moon;
A man went up in December,
And didn't come down till June.

The ram it had two teeth, sir,
Each like a hunter's horn;
And every meal it took, sir,
It ate five bolls of corn.

The ram it had a back, sir,
That reached up to the sky;
The eagles built their nests there,
For I've heard the young ones cry.

The ram it had a tail, sir,
Most wonderful to tell;
It reached across to Ireland,
And rang St Patrick's bell.

The wool of this rare big ram, sir,
It trailed upon the ground;
It was taken away to London,
And sold for a hundred pound.

The man that killed the ram, sir,
Was up to the eyes in blood;
And the boy that held the basin,
Was washed away in the flood.

The blood of this wonderful ram, sir,
It ran for many a mile;
And it turned the miller's wheel, sir,
As it hadn't been for a while.

Oh, the man that owned the ram, sir,
He must have been very rich;
And the man that sings the song, sir,
Must be the son of a witch.

Now, if you don't believe me,
And think I'm telling a sham,
You may go your way to Bervie,
And there you will see the ram.

100 O What a Parish!

O what a parish, a terrible parish,
O what a parish is that o' Dunkel'!
They hangit their minister, droon'd their precentor,
Dang doun the steeple, and fuddled the bell.

Though the steeple was doun, the Kirk was still staunin',
They biggit a lum whaur the bell used to hang;
A stell-pat they gat, and they brewed Hieland whisky,
On Sundays they drank it, and ranted and sang.

O what a parish *etc*

O had you but seen how gracefu' it lookit,
To see the cramm'd pews sae socially join;
Macdonald the piper stuck up in the poopit,
He made the pipes skirl out music divine.

O what a parish *etc*

When the heart-cheerin' spirit had mounted the garret,
To a ball on the green they a' did adjourn;
Maids wi' their coats kilted, they steppit and liltit,
When tired they shook hands, and a' hame did return.

O what a parish *etc*

Wad the kirks a' owre Britain haud sic social meetins,
Nae warnin' they'd need from a far-tinklin' bell;
For true love and friendship wad ca' them thegither,
Far better than roarin' o' horrors o' hell.

O what a parish *etc*

(According to A G Reid in the Annals of Auchterarder, the Parish of Kinkell, Strathearn actually suffered this fate — the minister was hanged, the Precentor drowned in the Earn whilst crossing from Trinity Gask, the steeple was taken down and the bell was sold to the parish of Cockpen, near Edinburgh; why the song features Dunkeld remains a mystery, apart from the similarity of the name!)

6

FESTIVALS

101

Blessed be the master o' this house, and the mistress
   also,
And all the little babies that round the table grow;
Their pockets full of money, the bottles full of beer—
A merry Christmas, guizards, and a happy New-year.

102 On the first Yule day

The king sent his lady on the first Yule day:
A papingo-aye;
Wha learns my carol and carries it away?

The king sent his lady on the second Yule day:
Three partridges, a papingo-aye;
Wha learns my carol and carries it away?

The king sent his lady on the third Yule day:
Three plovers, three partridges, a papingo-aye,
Wha learns my carol and carries it away?

The king sent his lady on the fourth Yule day:
A goose that was gray,
Three plovers, three partridges, a papingo-aye,
Wha learns my carol and carries it away?

The king sent his lady on the fifth Yule day:
Three starlings, a goose that was gray,
Three plovers, three partridges, a papingo-aye,
Wha learns my carol and carries it away?

The king sent his lady on the sixth Yule day:
Three goldspinks, three starlings, a goose that was gray,
Three plovers, three partridges, a papingo-aye,
Wha learns my carol and carries it away?

The king sent his lady on the seventh Yule day:
A bull that was brown, three goldspinks—
(the rest to follow as before)

The king sent his lady on the eighth Yule day:
Three ducks a-merry laying, a bull that was brown—
(as before)

The king sent his lady on the ninth Yule day:
Three swans a-merry swimming, three ducks a-merry
    laying—
(as before)

The king sent his lady on the tenth Yule day:
An Arabian baboon, three swans a-merry swimming—
(as before)

The king sent his lady on the eleventh Yule day:
Three hinds a-merry hunting, an Arabian baboon—
(as before)

The king sent his lady on the twelfth Yule day:
Three maids a-merry dancing—
(as before)

The king sent his lady on the thirteenth Yule day:
Three stalks o' merry corn, three maids a-merry dancing,
Three hinds a-merry hunting, an Arabian baboon,
Three swans a-merry swimming,
Three ducks a-merry laying, a bull that was brown,
Three goldspinks, three starlings, a goose that was gray,
Three plovers, three partridges, a papingo-aye;
Wha learns my carol and carries it away?

103

Yule, Yule, Yule,
Three puddings in a pule!
Crack nuts and cry Yule!

104

Yule's come and Yule's gane,
And we hae feasted weel;
Sae Jock maun to his flail again,
And Jenny to her wheel.

105 New Year's day

Get up, goodwife, and shak yer feathers,
And dinna think that we are beggars;
For we are bairns come out to play,
Get up and gie's our hogmanay!
Wir feet's cauld, wir sheen's thin;
Gie's a piece, an' let's rin!

106 Easter – Pace Eggs

(Alexander Smart, 1798–1866, Montrose)

The morn brings Pace, bairns!
And happy will ye be,
Wi' a' your bonnie dyed eggs,
And ilka ane has three,
Wi' colours like the rainbow,
And ne'er a crack nor flaw,
Ye may row them up and row them down,
Or toss them like a ba'.

There's some o' them are rosy red,
And some o' them are green,
And some are o' the bonnie blue
That blinks in Mary's een;
And some o' them like purple bells,
And ithers like the bloom
O' the bonnie gowden tassels
That blossom on the broom.

Rea Neill

Ye'll toss them up the foggy banks,
And row them down the brae,
Where burnies sing to sweet wee flowers,
And milk-white lammies play;
And when they burst their tinted shells,
And a' in fragments flee,
The crumbs will feed the bonnie bird
That sings upon the tree.

107

When Yule comes, dule comes,
Cauld feet and legs;
When Pasch comes, grace comes,
Butter, milk, and eggs.

108

Hey-how for Hallowe'en
A' the witches tae be seen;
Some black, an ithers green,
Hey-how for Hallowe'en.

Craig McKenzie & Gavin Ross

7

MIXTER MAXTER!

109

Hiccup, hiccup, gang away
Come again another day;
Hiccup, hiccup, when I bake
I'll gie you a butter cake.

110

Monday's bairn is fair o face;
Tuesday's bairn is fu o grace
Wednesday's bairn is a bairn o woe;
Thursday's bairn has far to go;
Friday's bairn is lovin an givin;
Saturday's bairn works hard for a livin;
But the bairn that's born on the Sabbath day
Is bonny and blithe and wyce and gay.

111

Nip, nip, taes
The tide's comin in.
If ye dinna rin faster,
The sea will tak ye in.

112

Sticks and stanes will brak my banes
But names will never hurt me.

'Sticks and stanes...' Paul MacLaughlan

113

Of the marriages in May,
The bairns die o' decay.

114

When I was ane, I was in my skin;
When I was twa, I ran awa';
When I was three, I could climb a tree;
When I was four, they dang me o'er;
When I was five, I didna thrive;
When I was sax, I got my cracks;
When I was seven, I could count eleven;
When I was aught, I was laid straught;
When I was nine, I could write a line;
When I was ten, I could mend a pen;
When I was eleven, I gaed to the weaving;
When I was twall, I was brosy Wull.

115 Eye colour

Gray-eyed—greedy
Brown-eyed—needy;
Black-eyed—never blin',
Till it shame a' its kin.

Tongue Twisters

to be spoken quickly:

116

Here's to you and yours,
No forgetting us and ours;
And when you and yours
Come to us and ours,
Us and ours
Will be as kind to you and yours,
As ever you and yours
Were to us and ours,
When us and ours
Came to see you and yours.

117

Lang may Auld Reekie's lums reek rarely!

118

Climb Criffel, clever cripple

119

I sewed a pair o' sheets, and I slate them;
A pair o' weel-sewed sheets slate I.

120

The Gunpowder Plot will never be forgot
While Edinburgh Castle stands upon a rock.

121

Will ye buy syboes?
Will ye buy leeks?
Will ye buy my bonny lassie
Wi' the red cheeks?

I winna buy your syboes,
I winna buy your leeks;
But I will buy your bonny lassie
Wi' the red cheeks!

122

Cripple Dick upon a stick,
Sandy on a soo,
Ride away to Galloway,
To buy a pound o' woo.

123

I had a little hobby-horse,
His mane was dapple grey,
His head was made o' pease-strae,
His tail was made o' hay.

124 Marriage superstition

If the day be foul
That the bride gangs hame,
Alack and alace
But she'd lived her lane!
If the day be fair
That the bride gangs hame,
Baith pleasure and peace
Afore her are gane!

125

When I was a wee thing,
'Bout six or seven year auld,
I had no worth a petticoat,
To keep me frae the cauld.

Then I went to Edinburgh,
To bonnie burrows town,
And there I coft a petticoat,
A kirtle, and a gown.

As I cam hame again,
I thought I wad big a kirk,
And a' the fowls o' the air
Wad help me to work.

The heron, wi' her lang neb,
She moupit me the stanes;
The doo, wi' her rough legs,
She led me them hame.

The gled he was a wily thief,
He rackled up the wa';
The pyat was a curst thief,
She dang down a'.

The hare came hirpling owre the knowe,
To ring the morning bell;
The hurcheon she came after,
And said she wad do't hersel.

The herring was the high priest,
The salmon was the clerk,
The howlet read the order—
They held a bonnie wark.

126

They that wash on Monanday,
Hae a' the week to dry;
They that wash on Tyesday,
Are no far by.

They that wash on Wednesday,
Are no sair to mean;
They that wash on Thursday,
May get their claes clean.

They that wash on Friday,
Hae gey meikle need;
They that wash on Saturday,
Are dirty daws indeed!

127

The lion and the unicorn
Fighting for the crown;
Up starts the little dog,
And knocked them baith down!

Some gat white bread,
And some gat brown;
But the lion beat the unicorn
Round about the town.

128 Granny and the Weans

(Alexander G Murdoch, 1843–1891, Glasgow)

Auld Granny by the ingle sits,
A keen licht in her ee;
The joy o auld times in her heart,
The gran-weans roon' her knee;
Her muckle pouch they rifle weel—
Hauds a'things in the toon,
An wi a skirl her auld snuff-box
For fun is handed roon'.
>   They're a' sneeze—sneezin',
>   They're a' sneezin' noo!
>   They're a' sneeze—sneezin',
>   A-chee! a-chay! a-choo!

She tells them stories, auld an' new,
O feys an' fairy folks,
Grim witches wantin' ill-some weans
To put in their black pocks,
Wee, tricky dwarfs, an' giants big,
Wha roam'd the kintra roon',
John Gilpin an' Dick Whittington,
O muckle London toon—
>   They're a' list—listenin',
>   They're a' listenin' noo;
>   They're a' list—listenin',
>   An' think the stories true.

She tells them o' the wee, wee wife
Wha lived within a shoe,
Of Mother Hubbard an' her dog,
The house that Jack built, too;
The cat that play'd the fiddle fine,
The dish that chased the spoon,
The dog that laucht to see the fun,
The cow that jump't the moon.
>   They're a' lauch—lauchin',
>   They're a' lauchin' noo;
>   They're a' lauch—lauchin',
>   A merry-hearted crew.

An' then, wi' serious voice an' low,
Auld Granny, thin an' boo'd,
Gie's them advice o' guid intent,
As wise auld grannies should.
She strips them o' their duddie claes,
Syne, when their prayers are said,
She leads the tottums, han' in han',
Each to its ain wee bed.
>   They're a' sleep—sleepin',
>   They're a' sleepin' noo;
>   An' Granny, wearit wi' her wark,
>   Belyve is sleepin' too!

129 St Andrews Fair

That at auld St Andrews fair,
A' the souters maun be there—
A' the souters, and the souters' seed,
And a' them that birse the thread;
Souters out o' Mar,
Souters twice as far,
Souters out o' Gorty,
Souters five-and-forty,
Souters out o' Peterhead,
Wi' deil a tooth in a' their head,
Riving at the auld bend leather...

130

Multiplication is a vexation;
Division is as bad;
The Rule of Three it vexes me;
And Fractions put me mad.

131

Shoudy, Poudy
A pair o' new sheen,
Up the Gallowgate,
Doon the Green

132

Evie-ovie,
Ca the ropie over,
Mother in the market
Selling penny baskets
Baby in the cradle
Playin wi' a ladle.

133

Nivvy, nivvy, nack, nack,
Which han' will ye tak?
Tak ane, tak twa,
Tak the best o' them a'.

Nievie, nievie, nick, nack,
Which han' will ye tak?
Tak the richt, or tak the wrang,
I'll beguile ye if I can.

134 A school rhyme about a house and garden

First in the garden is a raw
Of elder bushes fit to blaw,
A bed o' balm, and a bed o' mint,
A broken pot, and flowers in't;
A currant bush and a codlin tree,
A little rue and rosemarie;
A row or twa o' beans and peas,
A guinea-hen and a hive o' bees.
A mufty tufty bantam cock,
A garden gate without a lock;

A dial cut upon a stone,
A wooden bench to sit upon.
The house is neat, and pretty squat,
It's safer in the storm for that.
A looking window through the latch,
A broken door and a wooden catch;
And for the knocker there is a foot
Of poor dead Pompey tied to't,
So that they may remember him,
Whenever they go out and in!

House + the Garden.

Shelley Robertson & Claire Wetherly

8

GRACES

135

Hurly, hurly roon the table,
Eat as muckle as you're able;
Eat muckle, pooch nane,
Hurly, hurly. Amen.

136

Madam Poussie's coming hame;
Riding on a gray stane.
What's to the supper?
Pease brose and butter.

Wha'll say the grace?
I'll say the grace —
Leviticus, Levaticus,
Taste, taste, taste.

137

Bless the sheep for Dauvid's sake, he herdit sheep
    himsel;
Bless the fish for Peter's sake, he gruppit fish himsel;
Bless the soo for Satan's sake, he was yince a soo
    himsel.

138 The Covenanter's Grace

Some hae meat that canna eat,
And some wad eat that want it;
But we hae meat, and we can eat,
For with the Lord be thankit!

(Sometimes attributed to Burns, but the Covenanter's Grace was recorded in the South West of Scotland before the days of Burns. Robert Chambers)

139

Frae ghaisties and ghoulies,
An' lang-leggity beasties,
An' evil spirits, an' a' things
That gang bump i' the nicht,
Guid Lord, deliver us!

William Kirton

57

Selected Glossary

aboon	*above*	dicht	*clean, wipe*	lift	*sky, heavens*
airn	*iron*	doo	*dove*	maist	*most*
atween	*between*	douce	*sweet, loveable*	meal-poke	*bag for holding oatmeal/alms*
baith	*both*	drouth	*drought*	mear	*mare*
bap	*bread roll*	dule	*distress*	mickle, muckle	*big, much*
bawbee, baubee	*halfpenny*	fiercie	*a disease of hares*	mot	*old woman; mound; dust; speck*
big	*build*	flee	*fly*		
boukie	*body*	fleuk	*parasite*	mou	*mouth*
brenty	*steep, smooth (brow)*	fog	*moss, lichen*	moudiewort	*mole*
brook	*blacken, smear; marbles; sore*	gart, gars	*cause; make*	mumpin'	*mumbling, grumbling*
brugh	*halo*	gled	*kite (bird)*	mune	*moon*
busk	*get ready, prepare*	greet	*cry*	nane	*none, neither*
byke	*nest*	grice	*pig*	nane	*none*
campstairie, campstarie	*unruly*	gudeman	*master*	nebbie	*nose*
		gudewife	*mistress*	owsen	*oxen*
chackie	*clicking sound; teeth chatter*	hantle	*large number*	papingo-aye	*parrot*
chafts	*cheeks*	haw	*berry*	peerie	*tiny*
chapped	*knock, strike, tap, mash, chop, select*	horny gollach	*earwig*	pooch	*pocket, pouch*
		hot	*pannier*	poussie baudrons	*cat*
clachan	*village, town*	howlet	*owl*		
coft	*bought*	hurcheon	*hedgehog*	puddy	*frog*
cowed	*cut*	ilka	*every; each*	pyat	*magpie*
cranreuch	*hoar frost*	jaud	*worn-out nag*	pykit	*pecked*
croup	*croak, caw*	jimp	*slender; dainty*	raw	*row*
cuddy	*horse; donkey*	keeked	*peep*	rottan	*rat*
daw	*a lazy person*	kent	*known*	row	*roll*
deuk	*duck*	kittlin	*kitten; to give birth*	sark	*shirt*

saut	salt	speld	lie flat	tirling	tapping
sic	such	spier	ask	truff	turf
siller	silver	squaik	squeak	wauk rife	unable to sleep
slae	sloe	steel-wamet	thick-skinned	whippie	hussy
sneck	latch	straucht	straight	winnock	window
snelly	biting, harsh	syboes	spring onion	wonne	dwelling
soopit	swept;	tae	to	wymie, wame	belly
souple	supple; cunning	tee	tie	yeuk	itch
souter	shoemaker	thole	tolerate	yince	once

Kayleigh Buchan

Bibliography

Chambers, R (ed), *Popular Rhymes of Scotland* (W & R Chambers, Edinburgh, 1841)

Ford, R (ed), *Vagabond Songs and Ballads of Scotland* (Alexander Gardner, Paisley, 1904)

Ford, R (ed), *Ballads of Bairnhood* (Alexander Gardner, Paisley, 1913)

Ford, R (ed), *Children's Rhymes, Games, Songs and Stories* (Alexander Gardner, Paisley, undated)

Kamm, A & Dunlop, E (eds), *Scottish Traditional Rhymes* (Richard Drew Publishing, Glasgow, 1985)

Macdonald, A & Brison, I (eds), *Ram Tam Toosh* (Oliver & Boyd, Edinburgh, 1982)

Montgomerie, N & W (ed), *The Hogarth Book of Scottish Nursery Rhymes* (The Hogarth Press, London, 1964)

Opie, I & P (eds), *The Oxford Dictionary of Nursery Rhymes* (Oxford, 1977)

Further reading:

For help with some of the more unfamiliar Scots words found in this book please consult:
An A–Z of Scots Words for young readers   (Scottish Children's Press, 1995)

A large selection of clapping, counting, ball and skipping rhymes can also be found in *Classic Children's Games from Scotland* (Kendric Ross, Scottish Children's Press, 1996).

Well-known rhymes such as *The Sair Finger* (Walter Wingate), *The Puddock* (J M Caie), *The Whistle* (Charles Murray), *Cuddle Doon* (Alexander Anderson), and many less familiar verses, can be found in *Canty and Couthie: Familiar and Forgotten traditional Scots poems* (Anne Forsyth, Scottish Cultural Press, 1994)

For additional verse in Scots:
The Midwinter Music: A Scottish Anthology for the Festive Season (Marjory Greig, Scottish Cultural Press, 1995)
Teach Yourself Doric: a course for beginners (Douglas Kynoch, Scottish Cultural Press, 1994) and

The publisher acknowledges with thanks help received from the Scottish National Dictionary Association, Edinburgh who produce:
Concise Scots Dictionary (Chambers)
Scots School Dictionary (Chambers)

Index of First Lines

Ross Harper